Welcome

TOM ROWLEY

BACKSTORY Magazine

Issue 2
Summer 2024

Editor
TOM ROWLEY

Art Director
DARIO VERRENGIA
darioverrengia.com

Deputy Editor
MEGAN STELLER

Contributing Editors
DARBY BROWN
AMY STRONG
SAVANNAH SULLIVAN
DENISE WALLIN

Cover Art
MARÍA CORTE

Contributor Portraits
JORDY VAN DEN NIEUWENDIJK

Subscribe at
backstory.london/
subscribe
—
To stock Backstory or
advertise in our next
issue, contact tom@
backstory.london

Books and bookshops are too fun for hushed r... welcome to a magazine that bursts with colour

My favourite colour is grey. I like blue skies as much as the next pasty-faced Brit, of course, and I'm rather too fond of a loudly patterned shirt. But to make my heart really sing, give me a great wodge of grey. It's good bookselling weather, you see.

If the day is hot and sunny, browsers abandon the bookshop in favour of the grassy commons or the beach. If it's cold or rainy, they barricade themselves indoors, sprawled under a blanket with a book they already own – a lifestyle choice I thoroughly endorse, but one that isn't great for sales.

Mild and grey is the ideal, then. So I'm pretty lucky to live in London – not only the best city there is, but also surely the world capital of grey.

I've learnt all this in the last two years, since quitting my dream job as a journalist to pursue my other dream job: setting up and running my own independent bookshop. It's called Backstory, too, and sits on a busy high street in south London.

And inside, it's anything but grey. The bookcases are electric blue, the bar stools are yellow. The customers, too, are never dull. From the very nice woman who insisted a female colleague is my wife (I'm gay) to the regulars who are so much part of the furniture that we sometimes forget to throw them out at closing time, every day's a hoot.

We want this magazine to burst with colour too. It's a celebration of books and bookshops of all kinds. Long before I had my own bookshop, they were a constant in my life: places for inspiration in the good →

times, solace in the bad. And now, like most booksellers, I spend an unreasonable amount of my downtime browsing and admiring other people's bookshops.

We hope the pages that follow are lively, informative – and just a little bit cheeky. Books and the places we encounter them deserve that treatment: spark and playfulness, not snobbery or hushed reverence.

If you enjoy what you see, I urge you to join us on this adventure by taking out a subscription. You'll get the magazine to your door, anywhere in the world. You can choose to get the magazine only or to let us pick out a book just for you each month, too. And it's a great gift for your bookish friend whose TBR pile is so tall it needs planning permission.

Either way, please keep in touch. Sign up for my free weekly newsletter at Backstory.London. And drop me an email to let me know what you loved – and what you loathed – in this issue.

Speak soon,
Tom
tom@backstory.london

The Backstory team: Denise Wallin, Savannah Sullivan, Megan Steller, Tom Rowley, Darby Brown and Amy Strong

71 Balham High Road
London
SW12 9AP
—
books@backstory.london
—
Instagram:
@backstory.london
Website:
backstory.london
—

Contents

Contributors

ED CAESAR is a contributing staff writer at The New Yorker and the author of two books, *Two Hours and The Moth and The Mountain*. He lives in Manchester and recommends you read *Clockers* by Richard Price.

JULIA ARMFIELD is the author of *Salt Slow, Our Wives Under The Sea* and *Private Rites* (June 2024). She lives in south London. Her favourite summer read is *Into Thin Air* by Jon Krakauer because sometimes when it's hot you need to think about somewhere very cold.

FAYE KEEGAN has written for *The Guardian, Stylist* and *Vogue*. She lives with her husband and daughter on a narrowboat on the Oxford canal. She insists you read *Touch Not The Cat* by Mary Stewart.

ELLEN JONES translates books from Spanish. She is the author of *Literature in Motion: Translating Multilingualism Across the Americas*. In a heatwave, she'll read *Balún Canán* by Mexican writer Rosario Castellanos.

MARÍA CORTE is a visual artist who lives in Barcelona. She loves reading, art and red wine. She recommends John Cheever's best-known short story, 'The Swimmer', which is perfect for the suffocating days of summer.

JORDY VAN DEN NIEUWENDIJK is a Dutch artist who lives in Melbourne. He has worked for Apple, *The New York Times* and *Vogue*. His favourite read is *High Diver* by Michael Wishart.

HOLLIE MCNISH is a poet. She is the author of three poetry collections, three poetry-prose non-fiction books and two plays. She always reads non-fiction on holiday because she gets very excited learning about the world.

ANDREW BUNCOMBE has reported from 40 countries and every American state. He lives in Seattle where he and his wife are smitten by the natural beauty of the Pacific Northwest. He keeps *Hiking Washington: A Guide to the State's Greatest Adventures* close to hand.

ALICE VINCENT is the author of *Why Women Grow: Stories of Soil, Sisterhood and Survival* and *Rootbound: Rewilding a Life*. She lives in South London and takes the latest Emily Henry on holiday.

REBECCA REID is the author of *Perfect Liars, Truth Hurts, Two Wrongs, The Will* and *The Power of Rude*. She is a columnist for the i paper and lives in Balham with her toddler, Margot. She suggests you try *Unsticky* by Sarra Manning.

RALPH JONES is a journalist and comedy writer. His favourite summer reading experience was in 2003 when he read *Something Like Fire*, a compendium of posthumous reflections on Peter Cook. He claims that "something like fire" is now a tattoo on his chest.

RORY MCNEILL was Backstory's bookshop manager until March 2024. He has also written for The Telegraph. He implores you to read *I Will Greet The Sun Again*.

YAEL VAN DER WOUDEN is a writer and teacher from misty-grey Utrecht who misses the sun desperately. *The Safekeep* (May 2024) is her debut novel. She prescribes *Maurice* by E.M. Forster.

VIC SAUTTER is a Balham local and a regular in our bookshop. She worked in telly for a decade before moving into books last year. Her favourite summer read is *The Seven Deaths of Evelyn Hardcastle* by Stuart Turton.

ELOISE STARK is a freelance journalist and full-time traveller. In her free time, you'll find her hiking, snowboarding or climbing. She has a bone to pick with Paul Murray: she got sunburnt reading *The Bee Sting* on the beach because she couldn't tear herself away.

RACHAEL HANEL teaches creative nonfiction at Minnesota State University, Mankato. She is the author of *Not the Camilla We Know* and *We'll Be The Last Ones To Let You Down*. At least once a year she re-reads *Bridge to Terabithia* by Katherine Paterson.

KATE GRAY writes thrillers, including *The Honeymoon* and *The Summer Party*. She lives in North Yorkshire with her husband, children and two rescue cats. She takes anything by Lisa Jewell on holiday.

JORDAN AWAN is an illustrator who occasionally works as an Art Director at *The New York Times*, a position he previously held at *The New Yorker* and MIT. He is a professor at Massachusetts College of Art and Design. He loves Maggie Nelson's essays.

TIM SHIPMAN is chief political commentator at *The Sunday Times*. His quartet on Britain's post-Brexit psychodrama comprises *All Out War, Fall Out, No Way Out* (April 2024) and *Out* (June). His greatest summer reading experience was devouring the first three volumes of Robert Caro's monumental biography of Lyndon Johnson on the Trans-Siberian railway.

SOPHIE MACKINTOSH is the author of *The Water Cure, Blue Ticket and Cursed Bread*. She lives and works in London. She loves the heat and claustrophobia in *Picnic at Hanging Rock*.

DARBY BROWN is a senior bookseller at Backstory. She has also written for Bermondsey Project Space and Palimpsest Magazine. She spends way too much time creating elaborate meals. Come the summer, she loves comfort fantasy reads like *The Name of the Wind*.

AMY STRONG is a senior bookseller at Backstory and an assistant at literary agency Luigi Bonomi Associates. She likes bingeable books on holiday, like *Great Circle* by Maggie Shipstead.

OLGA PRADER is a Swiss-French graphic designer, art director and illustrator. She has published *Apartamento Cookbook #8: Tuber, or Not Tuber?* and *C'est bien*, a colouring book. In the summer, she reads *Mars* by Fritz Angst.

SAVANNAH SULLIVAN is a bookseller and marketing executive at Backstory. She lives in south London and loves cryptic crosswords and cheesecake. Her favourite beach read is *The Princess Bride*.

JULIA ARMFIELD

On reading and regurgitating

Not so long ago, I read an essay by Zadie Smith on the ways in which writers approach reading when they are in the weeds of their own writing. Her argument comes down to temperament – some writers, she notes, "won't read a word of any novel while they're writ-

ing...As they write, the world of fiction dies: no one has ever written, no one is writing, no one will ever write again."

Others – and Smith counts herself in this camp – need to read as much and as widely as possible, to take cues from a clutch of sensibilities and styles in order to form their own coherent language. "If your sentences are baggy", she writes, "cut back on fatty Foster Wallace, say, and pick up Kafka, as roughage."

I fall somewhere just south of Smith. For me, reading while writing is essential but what I'm able to read is strictly limited. This is largely due to the porous nature of reading and writing, the way the things I read tend to bleed onto the page when I work.

Rhythm, then, becomes a key feature of my intake – rhythm and a clean, measured pace. Books that I can (nay, must) reread while writing include *The Virgin Suicides* by Jeffrey Eugenides, *Blue Nights* by Joan Didion, *My Phantoms* by Gwendoline Riley and *Geek Love* by Katherine Dunn: none of them very similar in subject to what

I write, but each a masterclass in tempo.

Every so often, I'll go off-piste, and you can almost always find it in my writing. If I read something too talky, my writing starts to natter off the page. There are two pages in my latest novel, *Private Rites*, which are bewilderingly funny, purely because I happened to be reading Rebecca K Reilly's hilarious novel *Greta and Valdin* at the time. The moment I finished reading it, I ceased to be in any way funny, but I left the anomalous pages in as a sort of Easter egg for those in the know.

What, then, of the times when I'm not in the thick of writing? How to cope with the wide-open plains of possibility? In my case, I tend to get a bit weird. Since completing *Private Rites*, I have read not one but four non-fiction books on mountaineering, two horror manuscripts, a novel about time travel, one about Canadian separatism, Satanic panic and wine fraud and another about what happens when a whale gets trapped in the Thames.

As a writer whose drive to imitate is dangerously high, I can only imagine what would happen if I started trying to write with all of this rattling around inside my head. Presumably you will need to look out for my next bizarrely paced horror novel on wine fraud and whales, set up a mountain, to find out.

TEXTS

OVERHEARDS, MORSELS, TITBITS OF GOSSIP... WE'VE COLLECTED SOME OF THE FACTS GOOD ENOUGH TO MAKE IT INTO THE BACKSTORY GROUP CHAT

Virginia Woolf, whose not wholly genuine correspondence can be read on page 50, kept up a lively real correspondence with the feminist composer Ethel Smyth about a variety of topics, including these wise summery words:"How it liberates the soul to drink a bottle of good wine daily & sit in the sun." Cheers!

Overheard somewhere in Bloomsbury: "She's honestly such a lovely agent. She would always push her authors out of the way of the bus. I would probably throw them under it."

Misplace the book you recently borrowed from the library? Got a cat? Great news if you live in Massachusetts, where public libraries have been accepting pics of your feline friend in lieu of fines. The goal, to "get everyone back in the library", seems to be going down purrfectly.

Like your literature steamy? Head to Vinhan Kirjakauppa, a recently renovated bookshop in the gorgeous Finnish countryside. You can stay overnight, eat a hearty breakfast and attend an author event "in the cowhouse" (where else?). The best bit, though, is the bookshop's very own wood-fired sauna. Recommended reading: *Fahrenheit 451*.

Miscommunication in the stacks. In our bookshop, we keep customer orders organised alphabetically by customer surname. For no good reason, this baffles a surprising number of customers:
"I've come to pick up a book I've ordered. It's called David Copperfield."
"Lovely, what's your surname?"
"It's David Copperfield."
"Great, what was your surname, please?"
"It's by Carl Dickinson or something-or-other. It's just behind you, to the right. It's blue, I can see it."
"This one? Demon Copperhead?"
"Yes, that's right! You should really think about organising these alphabetically or something."

Publishing can be a morbid business, but things kicked up a gear when a book in the stacks at Harvard was confirmed to be bound with actual human skin. It appears that the 1880s French novel was originally owned by a somewhat eccentric (read: problematic) doctor, who took the skin from a deceased female patient in the hospital where he worked, without – you'll be shocked to hear – consent. Harvard intends to replace the binding.

5%

The proportion of overall UK sales of *Milk Teeth* by Jessica Andrews that Backstory was responsible for. Tom really, really likes that book.

Can I give it up now? You know the book, you're picturing it right now. The one you've tried seven times to get into, to no avail. Fear not, apparently it's fine to put it down, but do some quick maths first. Nancy Pearl, librarian extraordinaire, proposes: "If you're 50 years old or younger, give a book about 50 pages and if it doesn't hook you, give it up. If you're over 50, subtract your age from 100 and give a book that many pages before deciding whether or not to give it up."

Literary smut is in. The summer's biggest hits have sex scenes that would make Jilly Cooper blush. Not so David Nicholls's latest. His paragraphs usually make their excuses and leave at the bedroom door. A blushing Nicholls tells Backstory the reason is simple. He always thinks people would assume sex scenes are based on, well, his own rigorous research.

AROUND THE WORLD
in indie bookshops

Coventry Bookstore
Melbourne, Australia

This cosy book haven is a must-visit for stellar advice and inviting stacks of Australian and international fiction.

"*Everyone and Everything* by Nadine J.Cohen is a wonderfully candid story that made me laugh, cry and want to take up ocean swimming. We meet Yael in the wake of her suicide attempt and join her on a journey of healing that involves questionable amounts of dairy, dodgy erotic literature, late-night shopping, and the therapeutic effect of water. A beautiful tribute to family, to those with us and those that have passed on." – Emilie

Native Books
Honolulu, Hawaii

A publisher and independent bookstore, Native Books boasts three imprints. Pa'i Hou reprints out-of-print, rare, and beloved titles for their community.

"The internationally recognised nation of Hawai'i was illegally overthrown in 1893. Queen Lili'uokalani wrote her autobiography, *Hawaii's Story by Hawaii's Queen*, while waiting to present her case to the Congress of the United States. Her autobiography will help readers understand Hawai'i's complex history, the nature of her people, and their deep commitment to aloha 'āina – the continuation of a sovereign future which continues to inspire the people of Hawai'i that justice will indeed arrive." – Lise

We scoured the world map to find these bookshops we'd very much like to visit, and asked their teams to suggest a must-read local author. Get your TBR pile (and your passport) ready, because booksellers always know best.

Illustrations by Savannah Sullivan

Clarke's Bookshop
Cape Town, South Africa

Established in 1957, Clarke's is a city centre fixture. Set up as a secondhand bookstore, the beautiful shop now specialises in books on Africa.

"*The Frightened* by Lethokuhle Msimang is a tender and lyrical novella that draws on the author's own experiences of travelling, the work of healing, and what it is to find a sense of belonging. It is beautifully written, unconventional, and such a joy to read. *The Frightened* is published by Karavan Press, an independent publisher based in Cape Town."
– Jessica

Semicolon Books
Chicago, USA

Semicolon is dedicated to bridging the literacy gap among minority communities by providing access to books.

"One of the books by a Chicago author that my team and I love is *Last Summer on State Street* by Toya Wolfe. This book is a Chicago coming-of-age story about the things that force us to grow up faster. It centres on a group of friends living in city-funded housing that is set to be torn down soon; the story navigates the lesser-explored participants in a city's ecosystem in an honest way."
– Danielle

Shelfie

Alice Vincent

The bookshelves are probably the most beloved – and most contentious – space in our home. I used to live in happy chaos until I moved in with Matt, my husband, who alphabetises obsessively. Not pictured: the shelves in our office, which contain reference books for our work, and the Unread Shelf, our TBR pile at the bottom of the stairs.

SEASONAL   1
by Ali Smith

I marvel at these as a feat of publishing: four books written in real-time, published mere weeks after they were written. Smith's treatment of nature inspired me to include her and her wife, Sarah Wood, alongside the 45 women I interviewed for *Why Women Grow*, my latest book. The afternoon I spent with them in their garden was among the most illuminating I've ever had.

THE SHIRLEY HUGHES COLLECTION   2
by Shirley Hughes

Nobody captured motherhood or childhood like Hughes. These drawings defined my childhood and I can't wait to share them with our son when he's a little older.

We know that authors are well read, but Shelfie asks what secrets they are hiding on their bookshelves. This issue, we take a peek at the bookcase of journalist, author, and podcaster Alice Vincent. Alice's books paint a portrait of the type of reader and writer she is: warm, creative, and endlessly curious. Her bestselling exploration of women and their gardens, *Why Women Grow*, is out now in paperback.

THE OUTRUN 3
by Amy Liptrot

Matt lent this to me when we started going out. I ended up booking flights to Orkney and telling him he could come with if he fancied (he did). Liptrot's blending of memoir with descriptions of urban and remote island lives was galvanising for me, and inspired me to start work on *Rootbound: Rewilding a Life*, my first book.

ON BEAUTY 4
by Zadie Smith

Reading Zadie Smith is like slipping into a warm bath on a grey afternoon. I wrote my dissertation on her work, and have distinct memories of encountering all of her books. *On Beauty* is the one I re-read the most.

SMALL WORLDS 5
by Caleb Azumah Nelson

I read *Open Water* in three short sittings and it percolated in my brain for months – Matt lent it to someone, so we've only *Small Worlds* on the shelf. Caleb Azumah Nelson is such a deep and beautiful thinker; his depiction of love is searing. Matt and I adapted some of his words into a reading for our wedding.

TAKE ME TO

Backstory's booksellers cast their minds back to

● DENISE My holidays were mainly spent at home in not-so-sunny Oldham. I was a bookworm from a young age, thanks to my mum, so I spent much of the holidays in our local library. You could only check out six books at a time: I would max out my library card and within a day or two return all the books proudly, all read. I will never forget the grilling from my mum after a letter arrived from the library: they had spotted my "inappropriate" *Sweet Valley High* order, and I should consider it cancelled. Oops.

● DARBY When I think of childhood holidays, I think of the green-leaved forests of the Smoky Mountains, of white sand between toes, of warm ocean water. I think of how much I hated reading for much of my childhood. Only when I was about nine, when I read Harry Potter for the first time, did I fall in love with stories. Later on, I shifted into classics: Austen and Dickens and Steinbeck. I would wake early on family trips and read crouched in the hotel bathroom until everyone else got up, contentedly wrapped up in a make-believe world before the day began.

● SAVANNAH It was the summer of unfortunate events. Having discovered the sardonic world of Lemony Snicket in the first week of summer break, I spent my days in and out of Balham Library trying to get through all 13 books in the series. Unfortunately, they never seemed to have the right book at the right time: *The Grim Grotto* (number 12) sat on the shelf when I needed *The Miserable Mill* (number 4) and as soon as I'd finished *The Austere Academy* (number 5), *The Ersatz Elevator* (book 6) had slipped into the backpack of some other bookish pre-teen. Snicket's promised miserable ending (*The End*, number 13) remains unread.

THE BEACH

what they read on childhood summer holidays

● AMY The year is 2010. I'm by a pool somewhere in Spain. I don't know where exactly – I'm 11 years old and unconcerned with trivial details like my precise location. All I know for certain is that I've gorged myself on fruit for breakfast. The day is stretched out before me, blue and dazzling and hot. The pages of my book are beginning to loosen in the sunshine and the edges are lightly stained with strawberry juice. As the sun beats down, I turn the final page. I close my eyes and lie still for a moment. Then I reach under my deck chair and pull up my next book.

● MEGAN I was very lucky to be born to two dedicated any-time-of-night-or-day readers, who saw no difference in the books that you read midweek and the ones you packed tenderly in your rucksack to lug to the beach. Holidays in Australia weren't all sun and sand, though. There were also long stretches in the front yard getting sunburnt while painting the box the fridge came in, before retiring to the couch for several hours of uninterrupted Enid Blyton, imagining that I too could be a little English girl at boarding school, where I would (hopefully) get into endless "scrapes".

● TOM I forget why, but I graduated quickly from the first few Harry Potters to celebrity memoir. For a time, I was very concerned by Ruby Wax's ups and downs. On one summer holiday, I used my pocket money to buy Richard Branson's autobiography from the airport Smiths. I was about eight or nine and must have drawn some quizzical glances around the swimming pool. My parents were very liberal, but still. I might not have known what *Losing My Virginity* meant, but I can confirm it was a page-turner.

INSIDE PENGUIN'S FIGHT AGAINST AMERICA'S NEW CENSORS

Text by ANDREW BUNCOMBE in New York
Illustration by MARÍA CORTE

PENGUIN FIGHTS BACK

The incidents that went viral followed a pattern. At tense school board meetings, a parent would lean into the microphone. Sometimes they'd make a point of not reading out an explicit passage from the book under discussion that day, saying they did not wish to incur "condemnation".

Other times, they would do just the opposite, rushing through a line taken out of context, or misrepresenting a book intended to teach young people about puberty. To them, it was "pornography".

The speakers occasionally appeared genuinely upset. Often, though, the drama seemed strategic. How better to secure the Fox News headline that read "Florida school board forced to remove dozens of books after parents read 'graphic' passages aloud"?

When the chair would cut the micro-phone or ask the speaker to stop, as they invariably did, the meeting would descend into shouting.

For teachers and school officials, this was embarrassing, or perhaps infuriating. But for the supporters following along online (the meetings were usually live-streamed), it was just another skirmish in a far bigger campaign.

And the wind seemed to be blowing their way. "In Florida, we don't just think parents should be involved," the state's governor, Ron DeSantis, had said, after legislating to ban discussion of sexual orientation or gender identity in the classroom. "We insist they be involved."

IN THE GLASS-AND-STEEL headquarters of the giant publishing conglomerate Penguin Random House in midtown Manhattan, the suits are usually more concerned with the verdict of the *New York Times* than that of Escambia County School Board. What did that pesky reviewer say about Zadie Smith? And how many million should they print of the new Richard Osman?

But on the 14th floor, Dan Novack, Penguin's 38-year-old associate general counsel, was increasingly spending his time watching videos of these school board meetings, and he didn't like what he was seeing. Nor did his colleagues.

Of course, they'd dealt with book bans before – mostly by ignoring them. (At least one study suggests sales go *up* when a book is banned.) But this time it felt different. Rather than just querying one or two books, these protesters were demanding that dozens, even hundreds, be removed from the shelves at once.

Nor were the demands just coming from Florida. Novack watched videos of similarly tense meetings across the country, from Colorado to Connecticut, Idaho to Iowa. "It became mass scale censorship as opposed to localised," says Novack. As for the clips going viral: that, he reckoned, was "the whole point". "Get atten-

established a prize, awarding $10,000 to the high schooler who writes the best essay about how reading a banned book changed their life.

But for Novack, the biggest move would come in the law courts. Penguin soon joined other like-minded groups in filing two lawsuits, unprecedented in their nature. While the publisher has previously *defended* its books and authors in court, this time their actions were *accusatory*, alleging that a school board in Florida and the entire state of Iowa was breaching the constitutional rights of students, teachers, parents and writers.

Novack, who has worked for Penguin for six years, is mild mannered. He wears a soft blue sweater over a pink shirt with a Paisley-like print – more university professor than corporate lawyer. When asked to pose for a photograph, he pulls off his jacket and almost sheepishly pats at his hair.

But when he talks about the fight to keep books on the shelves, his voice sparkles. He calls the lawsuits "affirmative litigation". "It's a different mindset," he says. "We're dragging them in."

tion by eschewing any context, ratchet up the temperature, and make people angry and afraid."

The censors were gathering momentum. According to the American Library Association, book challenges in schools and libraries more than doubled last year to include 4,240 individual titles. Groups sent bomb threats to libraries; in Arkansas, the governor tried to introduce a law that could have seen librarians fined – or even jailed – for stocking "harmful" books.

So Penguin decided to fight back. The company set up an "intellectual freedom task force", with 12 staffers from sales, marketing and the legal team, including Novack. They set up a website with factsheets giving teachers, parents, students and authors the resources they need to challenge the bans. They donated to organisations fighting censorship. And they

JUST A HANDFUL of people appear to be responsible for starting this latest wave of book banning. The group Moms for Liberty started in Melbourne, a small town 70 miles from Orlando, objecting to schools forcing pupils to wear face masks during the Covid pandemic.

Tina Descovich and Tiffany Justice, the group's founders, say they're "dedicated to fighting for the survival of America by unifying, educating and empowering parents to defend their parental rights".

Others see it differently. The Southern Poverty Law Center, a non-profit that tracks extremist groups, calls Moms for Liberty "a far-right organisation...that opposes LGBTQ+ and racially-inclusive school curriculums". (Moms For Liberty did not respond to requests for comment.)

What is certain is that from its small start it has grown to occupy a powerful position, especially in conservative areas. Its fight against face masks rapidly turned into a battle against books. The group claims to have successfully backed as many as 500 people's attempts to get onto school boards, which in America have vast powers over the curriculum.

The group now claims to have 120,000 members and chapters in 45 states. And last year all five Republican presidential hopefuls addressed its national convention.

"Let me say a very special thanks to every one of the amazing activists and citizen leaders here today," Donald Trump told delegates. "You have to be an activist nowadays, because we're dealing with crazy people."

PENGUIN FILED ITS first lawsuit in Florida. Together with counterparties such as PEN America, a group which campaigns for freedom of expression, it alleged that Escambia County School Board was breaching two key amendments of the US Constitution – the First, which protects free speech, and the Fourteenth, which guarantees equal protection under the law.

The school board had banned about 1,500 books, including *Out of Darkness* by Ashley Hope Pérez, a love story about a Black teenage boy and a Mexican-American young woman set in 1930s Texas. Many of the books targeted by the school board feature Black or gay characters.

In Iowa, Penguin filed suit not against an individual school district but the entire state. It argues that legislation signed into law by another Republican governor, Kim Reynolds, has – as in Florida – robbed students, parents and authors of their rights.

There, Penguin has the support of the largest teachers' union, the Iowa State Education Association, and a father and daughter – Scott Bonz and his 17-year-old daughter, Hailie – who added their names to last November's filing.

Hailie, who has won prizes for her youth advocacy, is class president at Urbandale High School in Des Moines. Describing herself as an avid reader, she told the court she was being held back by not being able to read books such as *The Color Purple* – which has irked campaigners for its explicit language, gay storylines and depictions of violence – and *The Handmaid's Tale*, which is alleged to be profane and even anti-Christian. Books, she argued, "are crucial to explore ideas, develop curiosity, and grow intellectually".

Reynolds, the governor, focused much of her ire on a book called *All Boys Aren't Blue*, a coming of age novel told through the eyes of a gay Black teenager. "Our kids and our teachers deserve better," she told reporters. "They deserve the tools to help these kids succeed. Not a damn distraction on a nasty, pornographic book →

BACKSTORY

Meet America's most-banned author

Ellen Hopkins never set out to become America's most banned author. But in 2022, PEN America, a group that fights for freedom of expression, noted her work was the subject of 89 bans in 20 school districts. Nor was it just one title that critics objected to: the bans stretched to 17 different books.

Wearing the title as a distinction, she now intends to proceed with an even stronger sense of mission. "It's been exhausting, the last couple of years especially," says Hopkins, whose books include *Crank, Tricks, and People Kill People*. But "at this point, I cannot *not* keep fighting."

Many of the works by Hopkins, 68, are written for younger adults and focus on themes of coming of age. Often, her characters are queer. She says her works have always been controversial for some, and knows well the feeling of being challenged by a lone parent who had read "pull quotes" placed on a website, and taken them out of context.

But when Hopkins was first facing concerned parents, there were processes in place to help mitigate any fall out. Schools knew about the issue, and encouraged the offended parent to read the book in its entirety before engaging in a more robust dialogue. That would frequently be enough: "Often I could change their mind," she says.

In recent years the trickle of complaints has turned into a flood, in large part due to the organised efforts by groups such as Moms For Liberty.

"Now it's a handful of people behind all the book bans in this country," she says. "And it's a political drive, a political movement. They're not even reading the books all the way through."

Hopkins's books deal with real-life issues for teenagers, including sex, a wide array of relationships, and in one instance, sexual abuse. Putting these topics front and centre provides affirmation to young people who may be struggling. "We have to make it so fewer kids are suffering from [these preventable difficulties] by shining a light on the ugly stuff."

It is also crucial to Hopkins that young people know there is hope after any darkness they may have suffered. They have to be told "there's light past that, that you have to keep moving through," she says, referencing soaring rates of self-harm among American teenagers. "Some gay kids feel [compelled to self-harm] if they're not accepted… especially if their parents won't accept them."

She wants young people to know that they're more than acceptable – they're necessary – and there are "people that care". And despite the relentless flurry of bans, she has no intention of quitting. Hopkins knows better than anyone that this fight is far from over.

that should never ever be in a classroom." (Reynolds's office did not respond to requests for comment.)

But Hailie and her father believe they should be the ones to make the decision about what books she can read.

"It was hard to watch my teachers, who had spent years curating their classroom libraries and novels for [the] curriculum, essentially have to toss it all out the window overnight," Hailie tells *Backstory*.

"I was not the only student frustrated by this. People think that we as students are passive participants in our education, but we have voices and will use them."

FOR BOOK LOVERS, the good news is that the initial skirmishes seem to be going Penguin's way. In Iowa, a federal judge last December blocked key parts of the legislation signed into law by Reynolds, saying that the ban was "incredibly broad" and did not seek to handle the issue in "any reasonable way".

"Instead, it requires the wholesale re-

moval of every book containing a description or visual depiction of a 'sex act,' regardless of context," wrote Judge Stephen Locher. "The underlying message is that there is no redeeming value to any such book even if it is a work of history, self-help guide, award-winning novel or other piece of serious literature." (In January, the state's attorney general, Brenna Bird, appealed the court's decision.)

In Florida, a judge in January gave the green light for Penguin's suit to proceed on First Amendment grounds (though not on the Fourteenth Amendment). Both sides were readying for a trial as *Backstory* went to press.

But nobody thinks these are any more than initial victories in a long campaign. Least of all Novack's ultimate boss, Penguin CEO Nihar Malaviya, who is signing all the cheques. "He's like 'this issue isn't going away'," says Novack. "'It's only going to intensify. So we should get resources now and go big because otherwise we'll be kicking ourselves later.'"

Novack won't say how much the whole thing is costing. Or at least not apart from "a lot of money".

Still, if it ensures that students like Hailie Bonz can continue to explore the world, to grow up at their own pace and educate themselves how they choose, it will be money well spent.

Novack hopes people will join the campaign as they realise what is at stake and how much difference individuals can make. While someone might dearly wish to be able to end America's gun violence with a snap of their fingers, they cannot do so. Yet by attending school board meetings and demanding books remain available they can have a real – and potentially profound – impact on a young person's life, and on the type of society we choose to live in.

"You can make sure you protect your corner of the woods," Novack says. "This is a bandwagon... and people should jump in."

HOLLIE MCNISH

Justice for Insta poetry (& teenage baristas)

Another year, another flock of articles about how Instagram is ruining poetry. What was once an elevated artform is now obliterated by a glut of amateur, self-indulgent scribblers, they proclaim.

When people get so angry, it reminds me of the man I once saw screaming at a timid teenage barista. The teenager had the audacity to ask the man which milk he would like with his latte.

The five-minute rant that followed ended with the line *"Can you? Can you milk an oat?!"* If only I were still breastfeeding I would have offered the man some of the "proper milk" he was crying out for.

The same sort of unhelpful and unjustly targeted anger is often directed at poetry posted on social media. I've read numerous articles about how "Instapoetry" lowers the standard of this artform for all. I don't agree.

As far as I know, no Insta poet has barricaded the gates to university literature courses, lined up arm in arm outside Simon Armitage's Oxford lectures (free in podcast form online for anyone who wishes to learn from them – they're really great) to stop students getting in. They're not toppling shelves of classical poetry in libraries or intercepting publishers' emails offering contracts to more experienced writers.

What Instagram *has* allowed is for millions more people to access poetry; people who may never have opened a poetry book before, who may not have the means or confidence to soak up poetry in any other way. It helps people who, like me, grew up in villages far from live readings. For people who do love poetry, and always have, it has made it even easier to access.

Writing poetry has been one of the greatest pleasures of my life. Arranging worries or wonders into snippets of verse that I can go back to and shape and re-shape until I feel the page pulse has both thrilled and calmed me for years. I absolutely love writing poetry. Many people do. More people, it seems, than ever. I think that's a lovely thing.

Of course, there is a lot of poetry out there I dislike immensely. Every week I read or hear a poem – yes, often on Instagram or TikTok, sometimes in books or at gigs – and think "this is absolutely terrible writing". Some of them have been extremely popular with others. Then I think: someone has enjoyed writing that, and someone has enjoyed reading it, and that is okay. And then I step away, search for something I do adore and make a cup of tea.

I won't tell you which milk I use. I don't want any more hate mail.

SHOCK

AN ESSAY ON EROTIC WRITING

AND

Yael van der Wouden

REPEL

Picture: Roosmarijn Broersen

One time my friend B. got a dirty text from her lover while we and two other friends were out for drinks. It was a balmy summer night, and we were on the bar's patio – outside under a tree, angel lights on strings, everyone smoking. My friend was in a state about it: in the bellows of her desire for her lover, she could hardly focus on anything that night.

Me and the others were sympathetic and drunk. I myself had been stuck in the mire of a stagnant, one-sided love affair with another close friend who was also present – listening in, posture loose and eyes keen.

I said to B., "Why don't you just text her back then?"

And B. said, "Oh I wouldn't know what to text, what would I text? I wouldn't know what to text."

And I, brave with alcohol and my own unrequited love sitting so near, said: "I'll tell you what to text."

I dictated, she wrote. We were all flushed. It wasn't very explicit, that text. But it was purposeful, and it was dirty enough. She waited until our other friend went to get us another round of drinks to ask, quiet and intense, "Have you done that before? Texting like that?"

I had and I hadn't. My first foray into writing anything resembling erotica was at 14. I had watched a TV show, I was obsessed with the TV show; I went to the local library and paid €2.50 an hour to go online where I found a forum of other people also obsessed with said TV show. I wrote a little story about two minor characters making out and posted it.

I hadn't kissed anyone yet myself, though I'd thought about it a lot. I'd been thinking about it since as early as I knew it was possible – the putting of one's mouth to someone else, the pressing of bodies together. Mysterious and fascinating and something I couldn't wait to have for myself, and something I was terrified of just the same. The response on the fo-

rum was: "tongues don't bend that way when you kiss, how old are you?" I replied "20", and deleted my account.

Miraculously, though, I was not at all deterred. I tried again, and again. And then a friend gave me J. M. Auel's *The Valley of the Horses*. There was a phase, around this age, that I can retrace by looking at the spines of the books I read: there'd always be a cracked fold around where a love scene would be. I'd read them and re-read them, desperate for both the thrill and the comfort of it – the safety of experiencing desire only on the page.

By the time I was actually 20 the internet was strewn with my dirty little stories. I'd find a forum, post something, disappear, only to return months later with a new alias and a new story – the point was to do it, but to be untraceable.

Then one time, an online publisher of

Sleeping Female Nude by William Etty

erotica contacted me through a comment section to tell me: the work was good, and did I want to sign with them? I was terrified. I never answered, though I stared at the message often enough. It was fine, I thought, to do what I did in secret; it was another thing to do it in earnest, to do it with purpose.

I would circle that notion of purpose for a long time. At the end of that one night, after B. had left to be with her lover and me and my sad-love friend were walking home, the silence felt too heavy and meaningful. Then my crush joked and jostled me and laughed and said, "I didn't know you could talk like that!" I could've done something, then. Used those words that were apparently available, made them into action. Been purposeful about them. But I didn't.

There's a strange relationship, I've al-

ways felt, between the erotic on the page and the erotic in life, and what people expect having had the one – then the other. The fantasy versus the reality, the thinking about it versus the doing it. I once spoke to a friend of how I wrote my first sex scene long before I ever had sex myself, and what it was like to have had years of experience in the imaginary, but still be terrified of making it real. She was curious: "was there anything that surprised you once you had sex, anything that you realised you'd written wrong all these years?" My answer was so immediate that I had to take a pause afterwards, and consider whether I meant it, but I did: "No," I said. "Not at all."

Sex on the page is not about movements, I've found. It isn't about positions and who does what to whom – it's about desire. I still believe 14-year-old me could've made that make-out scene work, even if tongues don't bend that way, if I'd known more about building tension, if I'd known more about how to fan desire on the page.

When I teach erotic writing, that's the crux of my classes, of our conversations: desire. Desire and purpose. It doesn't matter how much sex you have or haven't had in your life; eroticism comes from a different set of experiences.

In fact, I've noticed that the people who come to class wanting to translate a lived experience to paper tend to struggle the most with making their piece work. They get hung up on physicality, on the who said what, who did what; they forget the reader. They forget that as a writer, you're not a character seducing another character; you're not yourself experiencing seduction. You're a narrative voice seducing the reader.

The first step of teaching erotic writing is teaching how to tap into desire, and how to translate that desire into words. In my classroom we always start at a step removed: non-sexual desire, non-sexual touch, non-sexual sensations. We make lists – things that we want to eat, things that have nice textures, things like good flavours, good smells. The next step is to find the contrast between those good things and the opposite – disgust. Bad sensations, bad textures.

We write sentences where the two are brought together to describe something. An example: *warm, leaking yolks*. What we're looking for is a balanced contrast, the sweet spot between that which attracts and that which shocks, that repels. We sit with the discomfort. Then we lean into it. We get purposeful with it.

The way I see it, that's where you find the overlap between the erotic on the page and in real life: purpose. Doing something intentionally, earnestly, doing something a little filthy and fully embarrassing with intention is where the erotic

> As a writer, you're not a character seducing another character; you're not yourself experiencing seduction. You're a narrative voice seducing the reader.

dwells – that hot tension between humiliation and want.

My favourite part of teaching is when my students realise that it's not the more literal sex scenes that make them blush, but rather the earnestness of an erotic text. Take, for example, Ellen Bass's *Basket of Figs*: "That hard nugget of pain, I would suck it,/ cradling it on my tongue like the slick/ seed of pomegranate." Or Carol Ann Duffy's *Warming Her Pearls*: "I dream about her/ in my attic bed; picture her dancing/ with tall men, puzzled by my faint, persistent scent/ beneath her French perfume, her milky stones."

These poems are far from explicit – not a single tit, not an ass in sight. And yet, it's never happened that I've read these poems aloud in a classroom without a collective blush rising up from the audience. Once, memorably, after the final line, a student whispered a breathless *"Jesus"*.

Erotic writing – be it a text to your lover, a letter across seas, a novel or a poem – is, I believe, accessible to anyone who's ever desired anything, anyone who's ever yearned or wept for want. The key is to be shameless about it. To understand the accompanying embarrassment as the engine that makes it tick; to understand that purpose is what turns it on.

ELLEN JONES

What's the Spanish for self-flagellation?

An occupational hazard of being a literary translator is that you're left with a bizarre and sometimes troubling internet search history. I just finished translating a novel about nuns, sex, and self-flagellation: *Apparitions* by Mexico's much-loved public intellectual, the 94-year-old feminist Margo Glantz.

It's a novel about the limits of the female body, the border between the sacred and the profane, in which three narrative strands intertwine. The first follows a woman, her lover, and her young daughter's perturbing interest in their sexual relationship; in the second, two nuns flagellate themselves, seeking definitive union with Christ; and in the third, the author of the first two takes on the voices of her characters.

The original Spanish was reissued in an illustrated edition in 2019, with a gold-leaf vagina on the cover. My English translation is due out next year, and researching it made me want to go "incognito" online.

Some of my tamer Google searches included: whether a litter of puppies has a single placenta or multiple; the precise difference between a whip, a lash, and a scourge; the positions in which Pasiphae, the minotaur's mother in Greek mythology, is most often depicted as having mated with the bull; words, onomatopoeic or otherwise, commonly used to depict the sound of a trumpet; and "do all breasts have areolae?"

The novel is written in short fragments with titles that include "The Dirty, Dark Red Mouth", "You Tremble", and "Her Greedy Thirst", which seem clearly sexual in nature. But as you read on, you discover that the mouth belongs to a dog licking blood off her puppies, the trembling is provoked by rage, not desire, and the thirst is for the blood of Christ.

Much of the novel is about the overlap between religious and sexual ecstasy – the border between the physical and the spiritual – so I had to choose language that could be interpreted in several ways, or risk diminishing the ambiguity of the Spanish.

One especially tough challenge was what to do with the oft-used noun "gozar", a word related to pleasure, sexual and otherwise. Glantz's repetition of it in the book's more erotic scenes creates a pattern I was obliged to dilute in English, because it was impossible to translate the word the same way every time; sometimes it's "I enjoyed it very much", sometimes "do you like that?", and sometimes "have you come yet?". I spent hours establishing every possible shade of meaning for this word, and you can only imagine the dark corners of the internet I ended up in.

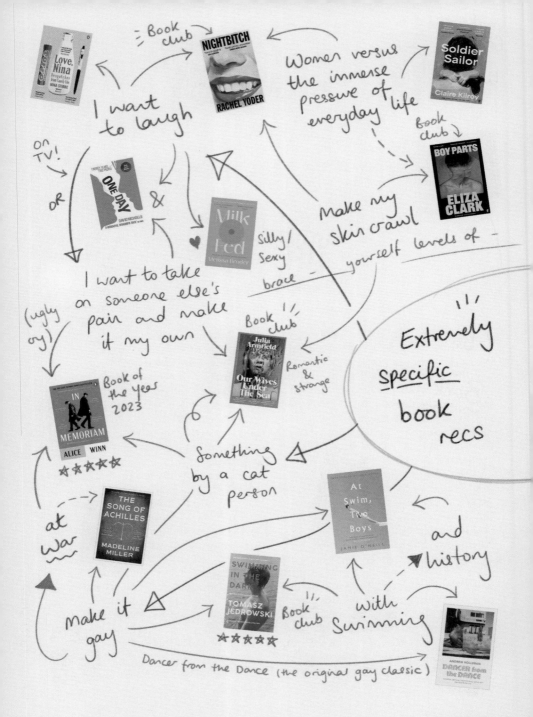

= Book club

NIGHTBITCH
RACHEL YODER

Love, Nina

I want to laugh

Women versus the immense pressure of everyday life

Soldier Sailor
Claire Kilroy

Book club ↓

BOY PARTS
ELIZA CLARK

on TV!

or

ONE DAY
DAVID NICHOLLS

&

Milk Fed
Melissa Broder

Silly/Sexy

brace —

Make my skin crawl

yourself levels of —

I want to take on someone else's pain and make it my own

(ugly cry)

Book of the Year 2023

IN MEMORIAM
ALICE WINN
★★★★★

Book club

Julia Armfield
Our Wives Under The Sea

Romantic & strange

Extremely specific book recs

Something by a cat person

at War

THE SONG OF ACHILLES
MADELINE MILLER

At Swim, Two Boys
Jamie O'Neill

and history

make it gay

SWIMMING IN THE DARK
TOMASZ JEDROWSKI
★★★★★

Book club

with Swimming

DANCER from the DANCE
ANDREW HOLLERAN

Dancer from the Dance (the original gay classic)

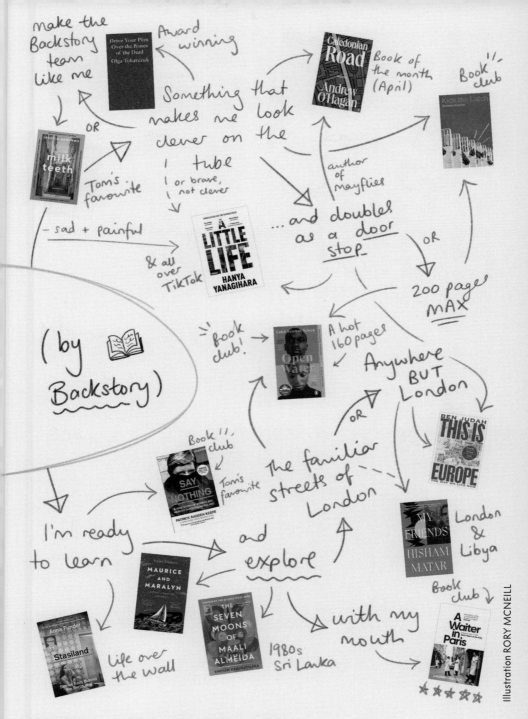

make the Backstory team like me

Drive Your Plow Over the Bones of the Dead
Olga Tokarczuk

Award winning

Caledonian Road
Andrew O'Hagan

Book of the month (April)

"Book club"

Kick the Latch

OR

milk teeth
jessica andrews

Tom's favourite

Something that makes me look clever on the tube
| or brave,
| not clever

author of mayflies

- sad + painful

& all over TikTok

A LITTLE LIFE
HANYA YANAGIHARA

...and doubles as a door stop

OR

200 pages MAX

(by 📖 Backstory)

"book club!"

Caleb Azumah Nelson
Open Water

A hot 160 pages

Anywhere BUT London

OR

THIS IS EUROPE
BEN JUDAH
THE WAY WE LIVE NOW

"Book club"

SAY NOTHING
PATRICK RADDEN KEEFE

Tom's favourite

The familiar streets of London

MY FRIENDS
HISHAM MATAR

London & Libya

I'm ready to learn

and explore

MAURICE AND MARALYN

Stasiland
Anna Funder

Life over the Wall

THE SEVEN MOONS OF MAALI ALMEIDA
SHEHAN KARUNATILAKA

1980s Sri Lanka

with my mouth

Book club ↓

A Waiter in Paris

★ ★ ★ ★ ★

Illustration RORY MCNEILL

EXTREMELY SPECIFIC BOOK RECS

THE BACKSTORY OF BOOKTOK

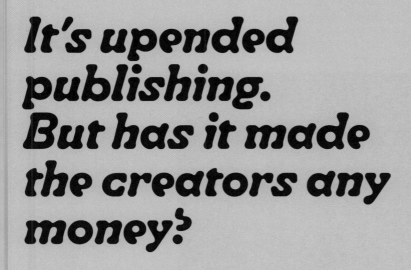

It's upended publishing. But has it made the creators any money?

by Darby Brown

Th/ere was a time when book-on-screen meant Hollywood. It meant vast studios and trailers and years of work. These days, it's more likely to mean TikTok. And instead of running their lines in a Winnebago, the stars of BookTok – as the platform's bookish corner has inevitably become known – record their content from their own home.

For Steph (@starrysteph), that means hunkering down on a comfy chair in front of a white bookshelf with rows of books arranged by colour. By her side, there's a knitted blanket and a pillow emblazoned with a picture of a bunny.

Cosy it may seem, but there is a steel edge to the impact of BookTok. In 2023, the UK fiction market documented its "biggest year of physical book sales" and "crossed the half a billion pound mark" for the first time, according to *The Bookseller*, a 4.5% increase on 2022's record. This jump is thanks in part to two of BookTok's favourite fiction genres: Science Fiction & Fantasy, and Romance & Sagas.

So it's great news for the industry, and for bookshops. But what about the creators themselves? What makes them tick? And does it actually make *them* any money?

BOOKTOK CAME ABOUT during the lockdown of 2020. The loneliness and isolation of the period, felt globally, pushed many to use the platform to find new avenues for community building.

Of the five BookTokers I interviewed for this story, all of them discovered BookTok that year as viewers and began creating content shortly after. Steph spoke about how she'd just moved to New York City to pursue musical theatre, only for lockdown to disrupt her career and her ability to meet new people. Brittany (@whatbritreads) said she discovered BookTok while living with her parents, having submitted her undergraduate dissertation online and finding herself with

stretches of newly free time.

Many of the BookTokers I spoke to have always been voracious readers, but several of them spoke about how the platform is bringing themselves and others *back* to reading after a period away. For those who had disconnected with reading – or perhaps never engaged with it much at all – a video of someone crying happy tears over a book could spark in them a desire to feel as strongly about a story themselves.

For these early content creators, gaining followers came relatively quickly. According to Kendra (@kendra.reads), all it took at the start was one viral video. Now, there are more creators, more content, and more direct involvement from the publishing industry, which, coupled with a changing TikTok algorithm, makes that kind of instant virality harder to recreate.

agrees, they negotiate a fee, and the BookToker gets to work.

According to insiders, publishers in the US typically pay big BookTokers the dollar equivalent of 1% of their follower count for each campaign they work on. For Steph, then, who has 130,000 followers, her base rate per post is $1,300 (£1,029) for major publishers and third-party agencies. Then there are add-ons, such as if the publisher wants the rights to repost the video on their own platforms, or if they want multiple videos about the one book.

It's not always black and white, though. Sometimes Steph will lower her rates for indie authors or publishers who she knows couldn't make that fee work. Conversely, she says with a laugh, sometimes big publishers will just throw out a huge sum of money. Who is she to say no?

Several British BookTokers I spoke with, including Holly (@the_caffeinatedreader), mentioned that creators in the UK make less than their American coun-

IT DIDN'T TAKE long for publishers' marketing and publicity departments to see BookTok as a way to increase sales. They started sending free books (often before publication) to creators in exchange for promotion.

Soon, BookTokers began to realise there was money to be made. The creators I spoke to all began making content as a hobby or a way to build their CV, with no aim to make money from their videos, but opportunities to get paid for their time and opinions started to trickle in before too long.

They can make money in several ways. The biggest source of income comes from sponsorships either directly with the publishers or through third-party agencies or PR firms. Often a publisher will contact a BookToker presenting the book they would like to be promoted. If the creator

terparts. Brittany, who has 56,000 followers, says that she makes anywhere between £50 and £450 on each video ad she makes for publishers, while Scarlett (@booksfortiktok), who has 5,600 followers, says that the most she's made on a video is £100. These rates, of course, depend on a number of factors, including the number of followers the account has, the publishers' budget and the amount of time and effort the creator can put into negotiating.

BookTokers are also sometimes approached directly by authors. Usually, these are indie or self-published authors who don't have the marketing and publicity support that others might. Creators might also receive offers of sponsorship from outside the publishing industry: recently, Kendra partnered with Spotify to help promote their audiobook launch, making $12,000 from the deal. Steph once partnered with Sherwin Williams,

> *In the US, if you have a video that is over a minute long and over 1,000 views, then after that 1,000th view, you can start earning about half of a cent per qualified view.*
>
> @STARRYSTEPH

a paint brand, to create content painting her bookshelf. She has also promoted TV shows, films and plays adapted from literature.

THE ONE PLACE it seems that BookTokers don't make much money from is TikTok itself. I asked each BookToker about the TikTok Creator Fund, which is a way for people on the platform to make money from their videos. Steph argues that although it is better than it used to be, TikTok is still not really backing its creators in the way they might hope to be supported.

The rules change often, but generally speaking, TikTok pays a set rate per qualified view, Steph says: "In the US, if you have a video that's over a minute long and over 1,000 views, then after that 1,000th view, you can start earning about half of a cent per qualified view."

As an example, she showed me a video that had received 500,000 views – one that she considered to be doing well – that she said made her only $200 through the platform. Kendra said that she hasn't even chosen to switch on the creator fund. (Holly alluded to the TikTok shop, a new way for creators to make money off the app by selling the books they discuss directly to their audiences. That could begin to change the game.)

Still, even though there are plenty of ways for BookTokers to make money from their output, it seems many don't – or could not – get by on that income alone. Every creator I spoke with either holds a full-time job outside of BookTok, or is a freelancer, with BookTok only part of their income.

There are certainly creators out there who could, and in some cases do, find their entire income on BookTok, but it seems many want to keep the platform as a hobby and any money made from it as a bonus.

Kendra mentioned that this is partially because she doesn't want to lose her love of reading. Importantly, all of the creators spoke of the freedom this allows them in turning down sponsorship offers that don't align with their values or reading interests.

When I asked about how they make decisions on which sponsorships to accept, they all said they would only promote books that they actually want to read and which were written by authors whose values aligned with their own.

Holly says that over time, publishers have become more aware of what type of books pique her interest – queer, YA, and fantasy. However, she and other BookTokers still turn down offers that don't feel like the right fit.

THE EXCHANGE WITH publishers goes both ways. Publishers are influencing the way books are talked about on TikTok. But TikTok is influencing the way publishers talk about books everywhere else.

Kendra and Steph both told me that publishers are using tropes from the platform to market their books and are increasingly focusing on emotive storyline moments, a clear change based on the way BookTokers review books. For example, a publisher might sell a book by branding it "enemies to lovers," a highly successful and searched-for TikTok turn-of-phrase.

It has geed publishers into offering big-money contracts to lesser-known indie or niche authors who might otherwise have struggled to be published. Colleen Hoover went from unknown to worldwide bestseller seemingly overnight. Without BookTokers "blowing up" the "romantasy" genre, *Fourth Wing* by Rebecca Yarros might have flown quietly under the radar.

Perhaps more surprisingly, there are also signs that the BookTok phenomenon is changing the content of the books themselves. Several of my interviewees credit BookTok with increasing the diversity of who and what is being published, since many BookTokers make a big thing of championing books that are neither by, nor about, straight white men. "It used to be there was just a gay side character," says Holly. "Whereas now there's not only a gay main character, but a trans character and a nonbinary character."

FOR THE CREATORS, though, the secret to BookTok is not to do with algorithms or tropes. It's something much simpler: authenticity. Not only do viewers see who is behind the account, they get to listen to them speak, watch them share vulnerable emotions, and connect with them in a way that other platforms, such as Instagram, don't quite allow.

Holly sees BookTok as the perfect blend between Bookstagram and Book-Tube (its Instagram and YouTube cousins). "With Bookstagram, there are pretty pictures, but you don't know who's behind the account," she says. "With YouTube, you know who's behind the account, but it's longer form, less accessible, and not as easily digestible."

With its short videos, plethora of content, and accessibility, TikTok seems to be the perfect medium to sell books. The importance placed on honesty and originality continues to draw in new and established viewers.

The BookTokers I spoke to were proud of their – and the platform's – accomplishments, from promoting lesser-known authors and pushing for more diversity and inclusion in the publishing industry, to introducing non-readers to the magic of storytelling. Many of the BookTokers feel these shifts give power

back to the readers.

Of course, the way we access and interact with social media continues to shapeshift from month to month. It is likely, then, that what we require from BookTok will also keep changing, impacting publishers, authors, and readers in new and surprising ways as it does. We don't yet know what the next chapter holds; whatever it is, it'll probably pan out as seen on TikTok.

What is my favourite part of BookTok? Community.

BOOKTOKERS

REBECCA REID

Books - like things - can only get better

Have you ever noticed how often you see the word "debut" used to describe a book? If you haven't before, I promise you will now. "Blistering debut", "staggering debut", 'moving debut' – it's absolutely everywhere, used as a synonym for new, exciting and undiscovered.

Of course, when I was a debut author, back in 2019, I had no issue with this. I loved the idea of being the new kid on the literary block. I chatted cheerfully about inking my first book deal aged 26, being snapped up by a major publisher when I was only a few years out of university.

Five years later, I'm a world-weary single mum. I am no longer particularly young, and I'm certainly not new. I have now published four novels and a non-fiction book. They have sold reasonably, but there's been no Dolly Alderton or Gillian Flynn moment. As a result of writing them, I am a better author, but I'm worth less – in monetary terms – than when I hadn't written a single word.

When you're new, a publisher is buying your potential. There's a chance you might be a big blazing supernova, so they'll put money and publicity behind your work. When you're a non-supernova with multiple books to your name, it's harder to suspend disbelief, so often your later books come out to little fanfare. That it makes commercial sense makes it no less depressing. Time and again, authors lament that they do the best work of their careers, but it's not their debut, so no-one notices.

So when a few weeks ago it was announced that Bloomsbury is going to publish my next novel in a big, exciting deal, several authors (privately, politely) expressed their surprise. While that might sound a bit offensive, I get it. No-one was more surprised than me. My agent and I talked extensively about how much harder it was going to be to place this book because I'm not a shiny new toy. My mean inner monologue still tells me that I had my shot, and that if I haven't done "it" yet, I probably can't, won't, or don't deserve it.

Obviously I'm biased, but I don't think any of this is ideal. So many writers became better and more successful as they experienced more of the world. Elizabeth Jane Howard published nine novels, to varying critical and commercial success, before the Cazalet Chronicles. Gabrielle Zevin had written ten books over two decades before *Tomorrow and Tomorrow and Tomorrow* hit the bestseller lists. How many brilliant writers might have made their publisher a fortune if they'd been given the chance for a genre change or shift in tone?

DECKS

& DESK

BACKSTORY

Last night, a DJ wrote my long-read: after a day at work, *New Yorker* journalist **Ed Caesar** puts down the pen and picks up the vinyl.

Illustration:
Jordan Awan

I'm 44, a husband, the father of two children, the author of two books, and a journalist for *The New Yorker*. In my spare time, I like to DJ, which might seem a surprising hobby for a writer in middle age who really should know better. I won't disagree. But I'm not the only hack at the turntables. I recently discovered that Aleksander Hemon, author of *The World And All That It Holds* — among other superb books — produces music and DJs as Cielo Hemon. We've bonded over our shared love of electronic music, and have vague plans to DJ together in Hemon's home town of Sarajevo.

I started DJing with my wife, who is a barrister, and who shares my musical interests, about four years ago. In the same way that some couples start taking swing dance lessons, we paid for a couple of hours' tuition with a professional DJ in Manchester, who showed us basic skills on the decks.

From there, we were on our own. We bought the simplest controller we could find, and started to practise. Pretty soon, my wife lost interest. I dropped deeper into the rabbit hole. Now, I play in a DJ collective called Beach House MCR, with two local friends who also should know better.

We mostly play afro house and deep house, which is what I like to listen to. Sometimes, people ask us to play at bars or clubs or private parties. We've performed at one festival: Bluedot. That afternoon, playing sunny house music while my kids ran around the DJ booth, was among the happiest experiences of my life.

In its simplest form, the role of the DJ is to select a track, then mix it seamlessly with the next. The idea is that a set builds. The great DJs can move you emotionally from one place to another from the beginning to the end of a set. The art of guiding dancers over the course of several hours takes years to master.

It also takes time to build a library. Modern decks use digital music files — mp3s and so on — and DJs have to possess the music they want to play. It's not like Spotify, where the world's music is at your fingertips and algorithms suggest what might come next. The DJ is the algorithm.

Moreover, the DJ has made an investment to build a library. Tracks cost about a pound each, online. It has been rewarding to curate in this way, having last possessed music in the iPod age. I can spend a happy hour ferreting around on the internet for tracks. It's like being a teenager again, scouring for CDs in Fopp Records.

The real pleasure has been in performance. It is consuming; all other noise stops. When I play out, it sometimes feels like those rare writing mornings when I glance up at the clock, and four hours have passed since I sat down, and I've written 2,000 words. Standing behind the decks, I need to concentrate on the technical aspects of mixing, while trying to cast ahead to where the set might go and attempting to read the room. Do people want to dance now? Or are they happy to bob their heads for a while longer? Do I give them something they know, or something I love and want to share? To be the motor of a party is a joy like few others.

(NOT)

STAR
GA
ZIN
G

WITH
MARTIN
MACINNES

WORDS : VIC SAUTTER

I have posted exactly one reel on Instagram. It was the night the Booker Shortlist was announced, and I was tipsy and watching live in a bar in Peckham. When *In Ascension* didn't make it off the longlist, I posted a picture of the cover, accompanied by Enya's *Only Time*, and the hashtag #yourestillabookernomineetome. The reel was quickly removed for copyright

MARTIN MACINNES

43

reasons, and now exists somewhere in cyberspace as a silent and ghostly tribute to one of the strangest, most beautiful and profound novels I've ever read.

When I meet Martin MacInnes, its author, on a rainy (cloudy), chilly (cloudy), grey (really very cloudy) day at Carlisle train station this is the first thing I tell him. It's partly to explain to him why I've been asked to accompany him on this stargazing trip, and partly to articulate to him how much I loved the book. It's all very well to love to the point of invention, but can you love to the point of cringe?

We are taking the train along the route of Hadrian's Wall to Haltwhistle, where we will find the Twice Brewed Inn, located on the edge of the Northumberland Dark Sky Park. It's the third largest area of protected dark sky in the world, and the largest outside of North America. On clear nights you can see stars hundreds of lightyears away.

However, as MacInnes and I share starbursts and book recommendations on the train, the featureless grey sky out the window is ever present. But hey, at least there are lambs!

MacInnes seems very grateful and a little bewildered that I've made the four hour journey north to meet with him. The popularity of *In Ascension* still feels new to him. Neither of his previous books (*Infinite Ground and Gathering Evidence*) have attracted this kind of attention.

I ask him whether he thinks the inclusion of a science fiction novel on the Booker Longlist is a sign the genre might be starting to be taken seriously.

"I may not be as optimistic as you about how seriously a good science fiction novel will be taken by the mainstream press," he says. "I don't think I would have had that review space had it had a different cover, a different title." The book, he explains, was originally simply titled *Ascension*, which, I remark, feels a far more classic sci-fi title.

"I think [*Ascension*] would have been

in the monthly science fiction round-up in the *Guardian*, which is two paragraphs, but instead I got a 2,000 word review. I had almost 13 months of continuous coverage, of reviews. I don't think it would have happened if it had been a more straight-up science fiction novel."

MacInnes argues that critics of sci-fi often hold up the worst of the genre, which they'd never do for literary fiction. "When it comes to science fiction, our shorthand for that, our go-to image is the worst of it. It's really silly and ray-guns. I don't understand that when there are people like Ursula Le Guin and JG Ballard [to read]".

In Ascension, I say, is similar to all science fiction in that it is really about humankind's relationship with progress. MacInnes enthusiastically agrees with this, and I feel very pleased with myself at receiving a good grade in Book.

We soon discover that the Twice-Brewed lives up to its name with an excel-

What it would have looked like, without clouds and with tree. Picture: MIKE RIDLEY

"THINGS THAT ARE HORRIFYING ARE STILL INTERESTING TO ME"

lent array of Roman-themed beers ("Ale Caesar", anyone?). Over a pint, MacInnes reveals he is a big fan of the *X-Files* and weird fiction. He finds H.P. Lovecraft a little overrated but is fascinated by horror.

"Horror is one way to access that comingling of matter, which is where we come from," he says. "If we accepted more of that it would be harder to have ill-treated the rest of the world, which we have."

That ill-treatment is all around us: in the news headlines, and on the pub's doorstep. It's a short walk from here to Sycamore Gap, whose iconic tree was made famous around the world by *Robin Hood: Prince of Thieves* and generations of selfies by Hadrian's Wall walkers. Or at least it was: the centuries-old tree was cut down by vandals in September last year, prompting headlines across Britain.

At the Twice Brewed, the spectre of the tree is everywhere. It's in every picture on the walls, embossed on the pint glasses in

"I NEVER FEEL WORSE AFTER WRITING. WRITING IS AN EXCUSE FOR ME TO THINK THINGS THROUGH."

our hands, even printed on the curtains in my room.

This sense of something missing feels apt, as MacInnes's books often feature some kind of loss in the background – whether the decline of a loved one, or the destruction of the natural world. I ask him how he feels about writing about that kind of sadness.

"I guess I never feel that anything I write about is depressing. Things that are horrifying are still interesting to me. It's like speaking about them is less depressing than ignoring them, hoping that everything will be ok. So I never feel worse after writing. Writing is an excuse for me to think things through."

I see this attitude in action. When MacInnes realises how close we are to the gap, he immediately wonders if we have time to hike up and see it. It feels like that same impulse to confront that horror face on, rather than have it lingering in the background. However, our dinner is about to come out, and we have an appointment to keep with a, still very much overcast, sky.

With the clouds showing no sign of shifting, we are instead given a talk about what we could be seeing if the sky was clear – which, while interesting enough, does sometimes veer towards rubbing salt in the wound.

We lie back on repurposed sun loungers to look at a projection of what's up there somewhere above the clouds. The feeling in the room is a little subdued but the talk is, admittedly, brilliant, as we are shown how to find constellations in the night sky. At the end, I excitedly squeal "how do you find Delphinus?", like I'm requesting *Freebird* at a Lynyrd Skynyrd concert.

At 10pm, MacInnes and I leave the dome into a night that remains impressively black. There may be no stars, but it's still extraordinary to see how dark a night can be out here in this protected corner of sky.

Staring into that nothingness, I feel a kinship with MacInnes's protagonist, Leigh, on her own mission to find something just beyond understanding. As MacInnes says, "the delay of revelation is more interesting than revelation", and as Fox Mulder says, "the truth is out there". Which it is. Even if it's hidden for the moment.

SOPHIE MACKINTOSH

Can't look, must look: the pros and peril of reviews

Writers fall into two camps when it comes to their reviews: don't want to know; need to know. Many authors don't read any of their reviews, believing that is where madness lies. I can see the logic in this. There's a mantra you can recite: *reviews are for readers, not for authors*. Once a book is in the world you can't change what you have written, so why obsess over what people you don't know think you could have done better?

To make the decision to ignore your reviews is to release your book into a world where you only get glimmers of its reaction, if it is adoring and wide-ranging enough to nudge up against your blissful unknowing (or, God forbid, terrible enough to puncture your attempt at peace).

Unfortunately, I am anxious and neurotic, and so I can't imagine not reading my own reviews as soon as I get wind of them. I once accidentally took out a newspaper subscription that took me an hour on the phone to cancel, so desperate was I to read their reviewer's verdict. That review ended up being so bad that my boyfriend cycled from work to yell up at my bedroom window that it meant nothing. Another mantra: *tonight's chip paper*!

I am getting more relaxed, though. I still read my media reviews, as I would rather know what people are saying about me (as with any gossip). And anyway my parents are going to read them and relay every word: best to get it at the source. But I stay clear (mainly) of Goodreads, as it is really for readers, not authors. There's the ridiculousness of subjectivity there: someone proclaiming yours the worst book they've ever read straight after someone else declared it their favourite.

But if you don't read your reviews, you miss a lot of opportunities to hear people say wonderful things about your work. It's high risk, high reward. And I have a party trick to confess to, which is that I've been known to read out my one-star Amazon reviews to friends after a few drinks – there are some real stinkers, which are pretty funny with the right comic timing. Sorry to Bookfan454675 – I know you didn't intend for me to perform your indignation with such melodramatic flair, but here we are.

Facing reviews head on has thickened my skin. I don't think it's changed how I write, but it has made me feel less precious about the reception of my words. The best novels interact with the world and each other, without too much self-consciousness. That is what I'm aiming for, rather than validation. Still, it can't hurt to look.

REJECTED SEQUELS

Words ------------------------------------- RALPH JONES
Illustration ---------------------------- OLGA PRADER

AS ANY PUBLISHER WILL TELL YOU, IF YOU'RE ON TO A GOOD THING – KEEP GOING. BUT THIS CORRESPONDENCE UNEARTHED BY BACKSTORY SUGGESTS SOME FAMOUS AUTHORS TOOK THAT ADVICE A LITTLE TOO EAGERLY

→ FROM: CHARLES DICKENS   TO: EDWARD CHAPMAN AND WILLIAM HALL

Messrs Chapman and Hall,

What an unfettered delight to see the country taking *A Tale of Two Cities* so tenderly to its collective bosom. Thank you for your role in its publication and proliferation. The experience, whose effect in myself I would describe as positively feverish, has given me reason to believe that a follow-up would enjoy a similarly warm embrace. What say you, I wonder, to *A Tale of Two Cities Two*?

Some might perceive a further instalment in the same milieu as a sign that the well is at risk of running dry – that old Dickens might have no more ideas flapping about in the aviary of the mind. Listen to them! The ideas have wings and the well is wet!

I await your thoughts.

Yours in anticipation,
Charles Dickens

← FROM: EDWARD CHAPMAN AND WILLIAM HALL   TO: CHARLES DICKENS

Dear Mr Dickens,

We are similarly pleased with the success of the book. Such a success has it been that we wonder if it has affected your mental faculties. We venture that your proposed novel, *A Tale of Two Cities Two*, might be in grave danger of damaging the reputation of its predecessor.

Yours,
Edward Chapman and William Hall

REJECTED SEQUELS

Dearest Leonard,

I realise that you are sitting across from me as I write this letter. I realise that you are close enough to hear the stroke of my pen on this paper and that you are looking at me with concern as if to say, 'Oh no, Virginia – what are you writing about me now?' Nevertheless, I write to you with an enticing proposition.

You know already that *To the Lighthouse* has enabled us to buy a motorcar. If people liked the book, then why not give them another on whose success we could buy a second motorcar? And, if the journey to the lighthouse proved popular once, then why not call the sequel something like *Off to the Lighthouse Again*. I dare say we might very well be able to lay the groundwork for a Lighthouse franchise.

I look forward to reading your response, my dear – and to seeing you at dinner.

Yours fondly,
Virginia

Virginia my dear,

Marvellous to see you at dinner and awfully nice that you are also lying next to me in bed as I write this.

Dreadfully sorry to say that it's a no from me, my darling. I can't pretend to have your genius, of course, but I suspect that *Off to the Lighthouse Again* would not be a prudent use of our printing resources.

The title alone hints at a certain reluctance or even cynicism. I suspect that, after the sombre nature of the first, people might like something a little more cheery in the second.

Enormous fan of your work though. Just going to turn the bedside lamp off and get an early night.
Yours with love,
Leonard

Fredric and Roger,
All of the evidence seems to suggest that *1984* is a veritable hit. Some books might be more equal than others after all. I am pleased to see that the novel has found an audience, and I thank you for your invaluable role.

The book's commercial success does not, however, blind me to the ever-present plight of the writer and his need to have enough money to hold at bay the spectre of penury.

With this in mind, then, I propose that we act quickly: would you entertain the notion of a sequel called 1985? Place this one in an imagined future as well, naturally - but with a crucial twist. That's right - it's *1985*.

My suspicion is that the masses will love it. Please respond - this novel is too important not to be published.

Yours,
Eric

← FROM: FREDRIC WARBURG AND ROGER SENHOUSE   TO: GEORGE ORWELL

Eric,

We hope you are well.

We're delighted to hear that you are so happy with the novel's success. When we agreed to publish it, we knew that *1984* would be enormously popular. We know with similar certainty that *1985* would not. Please, please do not write this book.

Yours sincerely,
Fredric and Roger

→ FROM: JAMES JOYCE   TO: SYLVIA BEACH

Fair Sylvia,

Been wondering about another book. Quick book. Idea for another book is it a good plan might be who knows. Can't know. Who knows. *Ulysses* big success. People reading the book on buses in shops in libraries with bulging eyes. Their bookmarks clutched in their warm hands red hands hands with gloves. Think next book could be bigger and why not. Write it fast, get it down, get it out. Ah, I'm hungry.

Idea: here it comes now all of it: follow-up to *Ulysses*. *Twolysses*. Nice book. Nice piece of book. *Twolysses*. Do you like it what do you think a great pun no doubt. Same stuff, mix it up, the people lick it up. Odyssey was a sequel yes it was as well. Sort of. *Twolysses*. Let's publish it. Iiiichaaaach!

Get back to me quickly get back to me true.

Goodbye,
James

REJECTED SEQUELS   51

```
┌─────────────────────────────────────────────────────────────────┐
│ → FROM: SYLVIA BEACH                            TO: JAMES JOYCE  │
├─────────────────────────────────────────────────────────────────┤
│ Dear Mr Joyce,                                                  │
│                                                                 │
│ Not all that easy working out what you were saying in that      │
│ letter. But if the gist of it was 'Do you think it would be a   │
│ good idea to publish a sequel to *Ulysses* and call it          │
│ *Twolysses*?', my answer is, no, obviously not.                 │
│                                                                 │
│ Take a breath. Inhale one of Nora's farts. In the morning a     │
│ new idea will come to you. Please never say the word            │
│ 'Twolysses' again.                                              │
│                                                                 │
│ Yours,                                                          │
│ Sylvia B                                                        │
└─────────────────────────────────────────────────────────────────┘
```

```
┌─────────────────────────────────────────────────────────────────┐
│ → FROM: CHARLES DICKENS        TO: EDWARD CHAPMAN AND WILLIAM HALL│
├─────────────────────────────────────────────────────────────────┤
│ Messrs Chapman and Hall,                                        │
│                                                                 │
│ Charles here. I have come to realise that you could be correct  │
│ about *A Tale of Two Cities Two*. I come to you with a separate │
│ proposition, independent of the aforementioned – what about a   │
│ sequel to *Oliver Twist* called *Oliver Twist and Shout*?       │
│                                                                 │
│ Yours in haste,                                                 │
│ Charles Dickens                                                 │
└─────────────────────────────────────────────────────────────────┘
```

```
┌─────────────────────────────────────────────────────────────────┐
│ → FROM: EDWARD CHAPMAN AND WILLIAM HALL     TO: CHARLES DICKENS  │
├─────────────────────────────────────────────────────────────────┤
│ Dear Mr Dickens,                                                │
│                                                                 │
│ Stop it.                                                        │
│                                                                 │
│ Yours,                                                          │
│ Edward Chapman and William Hall                                 │
└─────────────────────────────────────────────────────────────────┘
```

TIM SHIPMAN

Stick to governing - leave the writing to me

When I began work on my third book about Britain's post-Brexit political saga/ destructive psychodrama (delete according to taste), a member of Theresa May's cabinet declined to talk to me. "I'm writing my own book," he said.

Six months later he gave me a call. "Writing is much harder than I thought it would be," he said. "And it takes far too long." He handed me all his letters instead. Not for the first time, I reflected that some politicians are better at doing politics than writing about it.

We saw the same phenomenon with Keir Starmer. The Labour leader was working on an autobiography with Tom Baldwin, a journalist turned strategist. Months into this project, Starmer concluded he would be better off trying to win an election which he could cover in a future autobiography instead. The book became a friendly biography, published this January.

The relationship between politicians and books was most famously explained by Winston Churchill, who said: "History will be kind to me, for I intend to write it." Write it he did.

Churchill, at least, stopped writing during the war years. Boris Johnson, according to his aides, pined to take time off from governing to finish his biography of Shakespeare even as the Covid pandemic was beginning. Read Johnson's book on Churchill and it tells you as much about Johnson as Churchill. On every page the virtues of maverick outsider Johnson imagines in himself are highlighted. But the same is true if you read Churchill on his ancestor Marlborough, a lone genius in war who changed sides in politics.

Reading shapes politicians as much as writing. Johnson's spouting of the classics became part of his act. Denis Healey had hinterland to burn, making him attractive to journalists, but his propensity to quote poetry alienated less well-read colleagues and arguably stopped him becoming Labour leader.

Margaret Thatcher read little and subcontracted her memoirs to a committee of scribes. Tony Blair was more reflective, as his memoir, *A Journey*, reveals. It was clearly his own work and the better for it. Theresa May preferred cookbooks and Donna Leon novels and delivered a semi-memoir, *The Abuse of Power*, which showed she was no more reflective or inspiring a writer than she was a leader.

What can we conclude? That politicians who read are better at politics than those who don't, but that the writing is best left until they have concluded these labours. As for the history of this crop of politicians, they'll get mixed reviews. I should know; I'm the one writing it.

****

IN

****

COLD

****

BLOOD

Rachael Hanel
on teaching prisoners true crime

On a sweltering August day in 2022, I enter the women's Federal Correctional Institute in Waseca, Minnesota, one of 29 federal prisons for women in the United States. It's a low-security facility housing approximately 800 women, convicted of a variety of crimes ranging from tax evasion and money laundering to drug possession and homicide.

I'm here to teach a college course: Ethics in Literature, with a focus on works of nonfiction. We'll start with Truman Capote's classic *In Cold Blood*.

Prior to the course, it had been years since I had read the book. I remembered the main storyline: the murder of four members of the Clutter family in Holcomb, Kansas, on November 15, 1959, and the pursuit, capture, and eventual execution of the killers, Richard Hickock and Perry Smith. But what I hadn't remembered: how much of the book paints an empathetic portrait of Smith.

Smith first appears just a few pages into the book. Capote introduces him as an adventurer, a world traveller, flitting between Alaska, Hawaii, Japan, and Hong Kong. We learn that he likes to write, draw, and sing: he envisions himself as an entertainer and has already thought of a stage name: Perry O'Parsons. Capote describes him: "dark, moist eyes"; "pink lips and a perky nose"; "a quality of roguish animation."

Capote waits until the end of the book to reveal the gruesome facts of the crime. Only after we've read a detailed description of Smith's backstory do we learn that Smith was the shooter. With intent, Capote portrays Smith as a human first, then a criminal.

THE FEDERAL FACILITY in Waseca, like so many prisons in the United States, sits on the outskirts of a small town in a rural area, far away from an urban centre. We build our prisons out of sight, making it easy to ignore the humans inside the walls.

The classroom in the Waseca prison looks like any other classroom. Students sit two to a table. There's a whiteboard at the front of the room. When I walk in, 14 sets of eyes focus on me. The women smile; the room teems with warmth and energy. To me, these women are students first and foremost. I don't care what they've done to get here, and I don't need to know.

Truth be told, I did not see the irony

of bringing a true crime book into a prison class until after the class started. I had viewed the book solely in terms of the ethics involved in writing nonfiction. The book violates several tenets of traditional journalism: sources aren't clear, Capote recreates reams of dialogue, he surmises what members of the Clutter family were thinking on their last day, and the final scene comes straight from Capote's imagination.

But immediately, my students grasp the extraordinarily full, complete portrait Capote paints of Smith. A traditional reporter works to keep a line between professional and personal. But by all accounts, Capote developed a close bond with Smith.

According to many people who knew Capote, he saw something of himself in Smith. Both were short. Both endured brutal childhoods featuring parental abandonment. Both were intelligent with a propensity for wordsmithing. Both were gay.

To this day, the exact nature of Ca-

pote's relationship with Smith is unclear. It may have been nothing more than manipulation on Capote's part, the writer sweet-talking the young man behind bars, plying him with gifts and compliments, helping with legal matters, all in a bid to get Smith to tell his dramatic story. Others have claimed that Capote and Smith fell in love.

Whatever the truth, it subverts the traditional narrative. The women I teach expect a true crime narrative to focus on the victims, but the Clutters only make an initial appearance. The family is almost only a vehicle to get at the real story, that of Smith. "Is it ethical for Capote to portray Smith and Hickock with humanity? They are convicted killers, after all," I ask. I hear a chorus of "yes" and see the vigorous nodding of heads.

These women know what it's like to be labelled. For them, it's as if time stopped when they were sentenced. To society, they have ceased being a friend, mother,

IN COLD BLOOD   57

sister, daughter. Any good they have done before is erased. Like fossils encased in amber, they are criminals for all eternity.

I taught the class again the next semester, this time at a state women's prison about 20 miles outside of Minneapolis. This group of women also latched onto the relationship between Capote and Smith and again, we had engaging conversations about portraying those convicted of crimes with humanity.

I asked one woman from the class to tell me what thoughts the book brought up for her. She wrote: "The worst punishment that we can have is when society stops considering us as human beings and we become labelled as criminals, inmates, felons, ex-offenders."

In effect, Capote gave readers the opportunity to see Smith beyond his label as a criminal. George Garrett, writing in *Virginia Quarterly Review*, says Capote presents Smith with a "deeply dimensional sympathy."

I see some of myself in the women I teach. They are smart and funny, almost all of them avid readers. One woman is writing a memoir. They have made poor choices. I have, too. I have not committed a crime, but I have hurt people. I have not killed a man, but I have killed a man's spirit. I do not want to be defined for only those choices. I do not want the lowest part of my life to be the only thing people know about me.

After teaching the book for that first time in the Waseca prison, I went back to re-read Capote's epigraph. Translated from the French, François Villon writes in *Ballade des pendus*:

> Brothers, men who live after us,
> Let not your hearts be hardened against us,
> Because, if you have pity for us poor men,
> God will have more mercy toward you.

KATE GRAY

Salty language in novels? I swear by it.

"Cut the fucks!" my editor pleaded as I worked on edits for my latest thriller. This particular scene saw a character trapped in a room with a murderer. Surely anyone would drop an F-bomb or two in that situation?

Once upon a time bad language would get a novel banned. D.H. Lawrence's *Lady Chatterley's Lover* became notorious for its explicit descriptions of sex, its use of then unprintable four-letter words and a reference to anal sex, which was illegal at the time. Its 84,500 words contain 13 sex scenes and 66 swear words, from tamer terms such as "balls" and "arse" to stronger expletives.

None of this would make today's readers bat an eyelid. According to researchers, books published in the mid-noughties were 28 times more likely to include swear words than those published in the early 1950s.

There are plenty of examples of authors whose sales are doing just fine despite their fruity vocabulary. Bad language hasn't harmed George R. R. Martin's readership. The same with E.L. James's 50 Shades trilogy. The surge in steamy romance is littered with salty words.

You'd think that none of this applies to children's authors but Britain's former Children's Laureate, Jacqueline Wilson, got into hot water for her choice of obscenities. Parents complained about the use of the word "twat" in her novel *My Sister Jodie*, aimed at children aged ten. Her publisher replaced the word with "twit" when it came to reprint the novel.

Professor Sarah Coyne, of Brigham Young University in America, studied 40 books on the adolescent bestseller list and found, on average, 38 swear words per novel. That amounts to about seven swear words for every hour of reading.

Of course, it's important to use dialogue that sounds like real people talking. And a well-placed curse word can show the intensity of a character's emotions more effectively than a whole paragraph of description.

Yet, as my editor warned me, swearing too much can throw readers out of the story. Plus, the more a character swears, the less effective the shock factor is. Lee Child, for one, reckons the overuse of profanity dilutes its power and makes the writer look inauthentic. Jack Reacher might have notched up a bodycount easily into three figures but after 21 books, he has still to use the F-word.

You can't please everyone. And if you try to, your writing will suffer. But I took my editor's point and toned it down. So out came the fucks. Well, some of them.

Backstory of a new favourite

Alice Winn at Backstory

Our favourite book last year was *In Memoriam*, Alice Winn's debut novel. For good reason, much has been written about the book — and about Winn. So we decided to delve into the backstory of a less well-known person behind the hit: Winn's UK editor, Isabel Wall.

By Amy Strong

Alice Winn, Caleb Azumah Nelson, Jonathan Coe, Elif Shafak, Elizabeth Strout, Nina Stibbe... Chances are most readers will have heard of at least one of these names, if not several. But few outside of the publishing bubble will know the name of the editor behind their UK editions: Isabel Wall. "Good!" she exclaims when I bring this up to her. "I'm a behind-the-scenes person for a reason."

We're sitting in a nook of a room in one of Penguin Random House's two London HQs: there are plush armchairs, a coffee table, and a stunning view of London. Corporate but make it cosy.

Wall herself is well put-together with a calm voice and gentle demeanour. She is a proud Brummie, a background softly alluded to by her pronunciation of the letters "ng" in certain words. After graduating from Bristol University with a degree in French and Italian, her first foray into the publishing world was an internship at a tiny publishing house/bookshop in Paris which specialised in beautiful art books.

She followed that with a stint as a book scout, searching for exciting new manuscripts to entice editors, before landing at Viking, an imprint of publishing mega-conglomerate Penguin Random House, as an editorial assistant. Nine years (and several promotions) later, she's still at Viking, but now as a publisher, one of the big editorial bosses.

Unsurprisingly given her background in languages, Wall has always taken an interest in other cultures, a passion evidenced by the diversity of her "list" – as editors' rosters are known – which includes authors from almost every continent. In the post-Brexit climate of 2018, she launched Penguin European Writers, a series of translated "forgotten classics" with introductions by renowned anglophone authors, such as Colm Tóibín and Deborah Levy.

For the most part, Wall publishes literary fiction (her "heartland" as she calls

66
I'm a behind-the-scenes person for a reason.

it) and her list is home to an unreasonable number of my latest favourite reads, including the debuts *In Memoriam*, *I Will Greet the Sun Again* and *The Safekeep*.

These are books that explore themes I'm often drawn to: queerness, identity, coming of age and difficult relationships. But what underpins the fiction Wall publishes is the depth of the characters and their stories.

Many of the books at Viking were acquired at auction, i.e. other publishers also bid to publish the book but the author chose to go with Wall's imprint. Hearing Wall talk – about her authors, her colleagues, her job – gives me a taste of how writers must be won over (aside from the money Penguin can splash, of course... that's a different article).

Wall's keen sense of curiosity must attract authors with a similar inquisitiveness about the world. She recalls meeting Caleb Azumah Nelson before bidding to publish his debut novel, *Open Water*: "We ended up talking for a really long time about not only the edits I wanted to make to the manuscript and his hopes and ambitions for it, but also about books and art that we both loved and all these kinds of inspirations."

Editing is a "close-knit" process between author and editor, but Wall stresses that publishing involves a lot of collaboration between departments. Creative types, though, are known for their strong opinions and protectiveness of their work. Wall won't be drawn on disagreements over such matters as cover art, claiming: "We always try to find a consensus because essentially we all have the same aims for the book, we all want each book to find as much success as it can, as wide a readership as it can, and we want everything we're doing to be true to the book and to the author's vision." Maybe.

If her words have a slight PR sheen to them, her respect for her authors nevertheless comes across as entirely genuine: "A really joyful, varied part of the job is just spending time with so many really intelligent, interesting and creative people. I always feel I am learning so much from my authors."

As for what her days actually involve – well, not much editing. Nor reading for that matter, despite the romantic notions we might hold about such a job. She never reads submissions of new material during the day, but rather gets this – fun, yes, but surely time-consuming – job done outside of working hours.

Rather, in the cliched way of the corporate world, Wall's typical day is taken up with back-to-back meetings. She goes from acquisitions meetings (in which editors must convince the rest of the company to let them bid silly money on the manuscript they have fallen in love with), to schmoozing with agents to make sure they're on the go-to list for the next new thing, to checking in with an author on how their edits are going (although surely this could be an email?), to editorial meetings where the editorial team fills each other in on their projects (this could *definitely* be an email). You'd be forgiven for thinking that corporate publishing is more preoccupied with talking than it is with reading.

Still, it is easy to forget that a couple of years ago, we couldn't legally go to any

Who wore it better?

Many of the books Wall publishes in the UK are also out in the US. Which cover do you prefer?

Alice Winn
In Memoriam

🇬🇧 UK   🇺🇸 US

meetings that weren't digital. "Coming out of the other side of the pandemic, it felt like a renewed sense of how important those in-person connections are," Wall explains. "Going to events and actually seeing real readers respond to an author and ask a question and get their book signed, you realise how impactful and meaningful that is."

Wall tries to go to her authors' events as often as possible. "It is really interesting how you can go to events with the same author, but depending on who's interviewing them... that generates such different conversations and makes me think about their work in different ways."

Early events, just after the book has been published, seem to particularly interest her: "You're one of the first people to read the book, you're working on it privately, editing it with the author, helping them shape it to become the best book it can be and then everything changes and morphs into a more public sphere when the book is published and the reviews are out and there's a tour."

Again, though, she stresses she is much happier backstage. "It's my role to ask thoughtful questions of my authors, to guide them and to encourage them, and to nurture them over the long term. I don't think it's my role to get into the spotlight," she clarifies, adding: "I'm very impressed with my authors for doing that!"

Khashayar J. Khabushani
I Will Greet The Sun Again

🇬🇧 UK   🇺🇸 US

Hisham Matar
My Friends

🇬🇧 UK   🇺🇸 US

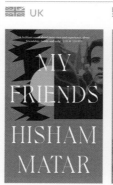

BACKSTORY OF A NEW FAVOURITE

EVERYTHING
IS JANE EYRE

So here's a truth that's yet to be universally acknowledged: everything – and I really mean everything – is *Jane Eyre*. Sure, it seems far-fetched at first, but once you're familiar with the signs (burning houses, unequal relationships, heroines whose anger and/or sexuality and/or trauma is so repressed it's forced to manifest as a mad woman in their boyfriend's attic), it's pretty obvious. Allow me to demonstrate (and please, beware of spoilers).

Daphne du Maurier's
Rebecca

An impoverished young woman marries a rich, enigmatic widower and moves into his massive house, where she's plagued by the memory of his glamorous first wife, Rebecca. Like so many bi-curious gals before her, she can't decide if she wants to be Rebecca, or be *with* Rebecca. In the end, she plumps for being complicit in her husband's murder of Rebecca. And then the house burns down.
Jane Eyre.

Thomas Hardy's
Tess of the D'Urbervilles

An impoverished young woman working at a massive house unwittingly attracts the attention of her employer – a rich, enigmatic rapist. She flees and reinvents herself elsewhere, finding an off-puttingly pious new beau, whose religiosity – like *Jane Eyre*'s St John – is communicated via the power of nomenclature. Tess is Jane if she understood Rochester for what he is: lechy, controlling, and full of himself. (Also, Angel Clare is the stone-cold worst.)

BY FAYE KEEGAN

Plenty of literary types claim they've seen it all before. There are only 20 basic plots, they'll say, or maybe it's seven. But what if rather than following archetypes, everything is actually just the same book, repeated over and over again? Because when you think about it – and Faye Keegan has really, really thought about it – everything is Jane Eyre.

E. L. James's
Fifty Shades of Grey

An impoverished young woman is seduced by a rich, enigmatic tech entrepreneur. He woos her with a first edition of *Tess of the D'Urbervilles*. Which is a... romantic novel? Anyway, she moves into his massive apartment, and he introduces her to his Red Room. It's kind of like the Red Room a disgraced Jane is sent to as a child, but the punishments meted out here are a little more extreme...

Pretty much everything ever optioned by Reese Witherspoon's production company Hello Sunshine

There's *Gone Girl* (a secret other woman; all that repressed cool girl rage); there's *Little Fires Everywhere* (repressed desires! A burning house!); there's *Eleanor Oliphant is Completely Fine* (another burning house! Repressed trauma manifesting as an angry, institutionalised woman!) Oh, and there's *Wild*, in which a woman takes a masochistically long walk and connects with nature while reflecting on her past moral failings – much like Jane does when she flees Thornfield after discovering Rochester is already hitched. *Jane Eyre*.

The complete works
of Taylor Swift

You've got unequal pairings ("don't you think I was too young to be messed with?"), you've got concealed relationships ("I don't wanna keep secrets just to keep you!"), you've got not-so repressed rage ("there's nothin' like a mad woman"), you've even got burning houses ("he's gonna burn this house to the ground"). *Jane Eyre* all over the place.

Beyoncé's
greatest record

Lemonade is all about discovering your husband has a secret other woman and ultimately deciding to stay with him anyway. I'm not suggesting Jay-Z had Becky With the Good Hair locked in the attic, but I'm not *not* suggesting it.

Postcard from:
TOKYO

Book and Bed Tokyo

As I crawl out of bed, I stumble into an American in a kimono, searching for the next instalment of his favourite manga. That is to be expected when the walls of your capsule hotel are built out of bookshelves.

Book and Bed Tokyo is a library, cafe, and hotel combined. When I checked in the night before, I instantly fell in love. The staff gave me some slippers and a fluffy blanket. The orange lights cast a soft glow onto the walls of books, interrupted by small curtains hiding each capsule. I left my rucksack in my surprisingly spacious booth and set off in search of some reading material.

One side of the room is taken up by a tiered sitting area with books beneath the seats and along the walls. Two people were already nestled at different heights. "It's great vibes, isn't it?" asked an American-accented voice. I turned and saw a long-haired man sitting on a velvet sofa. Above him pages of manga dangled from the ceiling, a literary candelabra.

Book and Bed is in the middle of Shinjuku district, a neon-filled, ramen-fuelled, jam-packed neighbourhood. The streets buzz with crowds of schoolgirls, businessmen and tourists. The air is filled with jingles playing over the loudspeaker and the clinks and beeps of pachinko parlours.

This is one of the city's most popular neighbourhoods, and most hotels are pricey. As the world's largest city and one of the most densely populated, Tokyo has to be creative regarding accommodation options. Capsule hotels are well known for providing space-efficient, wallet-friendly places to stay — although they often come with a certain sterility. Not so Book and Bed.

Yukio, in town for a business meeting, agreed. "Book and Bed isn't like other hotels, where you can feel a bit lonely. You can spend your evening reading rather than lying in your capsule!"

As the day goes on, the atmosphere changes. Groups of women come in for an Instagrammable coffee, selecting from a menu of drinks designed more for their goth aesthetic than their taste — black strawberry milk, anyone? A couple cuddles cosily in a corner, holding each other with one arm and a book in the other.

The introvert heaven of the night before has gone. I find myself longing for the evening when I'll grab a book and hunker down. **Eloise Stark**